LOOKING FOR TROUBLE?

Well, here he is! Young man trouble himself (and friend) getting ready for another round of those lethal laugh-busters that have been rolling his fans in the aisles for more than 15 years. That's some record!

Dennis anyone?

Dennis the Menace

FAWCETT CREST • NEW YORK

...Here Comes Trouble

by Hank Ketcham

DENNIS THE MENACE, HERE COMES TROUBLE

Published by Fawcett Crest Books, a unit of CBS Publications, the Consumer Publishing Division of CBS Inc., by arrangement with The Hall Syndicate, Inc.

ISBN: 0-449-13634-5

Printed in the United States of America

29   28   27   26   25   24   23   22   21   20

"NOW WE'LL *NEVER* KNOW HOW LONG IT TAKES A SNAIL TO CRAWL FROM THE KITCHEN TO THE LIVIN' ROOM!"

"MOM SAID NOT TO BOTHER YOU, SO I'M GONNA TRY AN' FIND ANOTHER FATHER TO BE A PAL WITH."

"SHE WON'T BE ANY TROUBLE! MOST OF THE TIME SHE'LL BE PLAYIN' WITH HER BROTHERS AND SISTERS THAT I LEFT OUTSIDE."

"YA KNOW SOMETHIN', TOMMY? YOUR SISTER IS ALMOST GOOD AS A *BROTHER!*"

"OPERATOR, DO YOU KNOW ANY OTHER LITTLE BOYS WHO FEEL LIKE TALKING?"

"BOY! WAS THAT LATE-LATE MOVIE EVER *SCARY!*"

VEGETABLE SOUP?! GEE WHIZ! WHY WOULD YA BE LOOKIN' FOR *THAT*?

"WELL, WINTER'S HERE. I JUST SAW MY FIRST SNOWBALL

"ME AN' MRS. WILSON PLAYED HER PIANO FOR AN HOUR AN' THEN WE HAD ICE CREAM. AN' MR. WILSON HAD TWO ASPIRIN!"

"I NEVER SAW MY *MOM* SO MAD..I THOUGHT SHE WAS GOING TO JUMP OUT OF THE TUB AND *SPANK* ALL OF US!"

"I'LL JUST LIFT THE LID AN' YOU CAN PEEK ...... *OOPS! THERE THEY GO!*"

"BUT THE KIDS I KNOW DON'T HIT ON THE CHEEK. THEY HIT ON THE *NOSE!*"

"HE'S MUCH BETTER, DOCTOR. IN FACT I DON'T KNOW HOW MUCH LONGER I CAN KEEP HIM IN BED."

"WELL, IF THEY DON'T *MAKE* YA LEAVE THE SHIP, WHY *DO* YA?"

"FISTS? FISTS ARE JUST YOUR HANDS WHEN THEY GET *MAD!*"

"SURE, I'LL GO WITH YA. WHERE'S FLORIDA?"

"I KNEW SHE WAS SICK WHEN SHE LET ME EAT LUNCH WITHOUT WASHIN' MY HANDS!"

"RUFF'S NOT THE ONE THAT'S BARKIN'! HE'S JUST *ANSWERIN'!*"

"MY PIPE HAS *NOTHING* TO DO WITH IT! I *KNOW* WHAT'S CAUSING MY ULCER!"

"AN' NEXT TIME I'M GONNA KNOCK THE *SOCKS* OFF HIM, TOO!"

TAKE TAP, ACROBATIC AND BALLET *NO* PIANO LESSONS!"

"THAT'S TOUGH."

"GEE, MOM, YOU SURE LOOK *WEAK* WITHOUT MAKE-UP!"

"IF YA WANNA WINDOW SHOP, YOU COULDN'T BEAT *THIS* ONE!"

"I GOT A RULE THAT I DON'T THROW SNOWBALLS AT PEOPLE WHO GIVE ME A NICKEL."

"EY, MOM! I GOT SHOVED OVER HERE 'TWEEN TWO SCRATCHY OL' OVERCOATS!"

"YA KNOW WHAT I LIKE BEST 'BOUT VACATIONS? *STUFFIN'* YOURSELF ALL THE TIME!"

"WAS *WINNIN'* 'TIL HE STARTED HITTIN' BACK!"

"LET'S *DO* SOMETHIN'.....LIKE RACE TO THE HOT DOG STAND!"

"JOEY ISN'T *REALLY* SHY. HE'S JUST *CAREFUL!*"

"*DAD!* THIS GUY'S ON *HIS* VACATION, TOO!"

"MISS BROWN! TOMMY'S PUTTING *WATER* IN THE SAND BOX! AND DENNIS HAS A LITTLE SACK OF *CEMENT!*"

"OH, I JUST HAVE AN AVERAGE SIZE BACKYARD. WHY?"

"WELL, WHERE THE HECK DO YA *GROW* ALL THIS STUFF?"

"HEY, GUARD! WE WANT *OUTA* HERE!"

"NAP TIME, CHILDREN! REMEMBER, LITTLE CLOCKS RUN DOWN...."

"NOT *ME*! DAD SAYS I'M SELF-WINDIN'!"

"...AN' PLEASE TRY TO STOP MR. WILSON'S WINDOWS FROM BREAKIN' SO EASY."

"I'D TRADE EVERYTHING IN THERE FOR A PONY AN' TWO BALES O' HAY."

"HE CAN'T HIT THE BALL SO GOOD BUT, *BOY,* CAN HE THROW A GOLF CLUB!"

"YOU TELL 'IM. THE POOR KID'S BEEN ASKIN' HIS UNCLE
FOR THAT GLOVE SINCE LAST SUMMER!"

"HEY, WHAT ABOUT *PILLOWS*?"

"YOU PEOPLE MIGHT AS WELL STAY UP.
I'LL BE RIGHT BACK."

"HERE, TOMMY. I SNUGGLED YA A BOTTLE O' ROOT BEER! A GUY GETS *TIRED* OF MEDICINE!"

"ALL RIGHT, WE'LL THINK OF A *NEW* NAME FOR ME. LET'S SEE, YOU DON'T LIKE 'BABY SITTER', AND *I* DON'T LIKE 'SKINNY'....."

"I'LL BET I'VE GROWED. THIS MORNIN' MARGARET CALLED ME A *BIG* BULLY'!"

"I PICKED UP A CHARLEY-HORSE
YESTERDAY AND I CAN'T GET RID OF IT."

"*I'LL* TAKE IT!"

"WHEN MOM GETS THROUGH TALKIN' TO MRS. WILSON, COULD WE CALL THE KENNEL AN' SAY 'HELLO' TO *RUFF*?"

"GEE, MR. WILSON, I DIDN'T THINK THAT CRAZY YO-YO WOULD DO A THING LIKE *THAT!*"

DAD! COME SEE HOW PRETTY IT LOOKS WHEN THE SPRINKLER IS ON ALL NIGHT!"

"HOW DID MY BOWLING BALL GET OUT HERE?"

"ROLLED?"

"ES, SIR, FOLKS, THAT'S WHAT I CALL A *CLEAN SHAVE!*"

"IF WE'D *ALL* GO TO BED WHEN *I* DO, YOU WOULDN'T *HAVE* SUCH A *BIG* LIGHT BILL!"

"BOY, A GUY WOULDN'T GET AWAY WITH *NOTHIN'*
IF HE HAD *FOUR* MOTHERS!"

"HEY, MOM! DID YA NOTICE I DIDN'T SLAM THE DOOR?"

STEN TO *MY* FORTUNE COOKIE: AFTER THIS DINNER YOUR MOM AN' DAD E GONNA TAKE YOU TO A COWBOY MOVIE, AN' AFTER *THAT*...."

"YEAH. I'VE GOT A LITTLE KID AT HOME. WHY?"

"HOW WOULD YOU LIKE TO SW— A ICE CREAM CONE FOR A *REE— FIRE ENGINE?*"

"WHAT THE HECK'S WRONG WITH KEEPIN' THINGS *HANDY*?"

"BUSINESS IS FINE. ONE FAMILY, NAME OF MITCHELL,
BRINGS IN STUFF ONCE OR TWICE A WEEK."

"...AT'S MY SITTER. BOY, SHE SURE TAKES CARE OF SOME PRETTY BIG KIDS!"

"BEFORE YA COVER UP THAT BONE, LET'S
THROW THIS *BROCCOLI* IN THERE!"

"DRESS SHOP. WHERE'S YOUR MOM DRAGGIN' *YOU*?"

"HMMMM. HERE'S A **VERY** 'PORTANT LETTER FOR....
SOMEBODY, FROM......SOMEBODY."

"HOW DOES IT FEEL TO BUST STUFF AND NOT HAVE NOBODY *YELL* AT YA?"

"WHATTA YA MEAN I DON'T KNOW ONE TREE FROM ANOTHER? THAT'S A *BIG* TREE! THAT'S A *LITTLE* TREE! THAT'S A....."

DENNIS IS WRONG, JOEY. THERE'S NOTHING SISSY ABOUT TAKING A NAP!"

"OW COME YA ALWAYS SEND ME TO BED BEFORE SSERT, AN' NEVER BEFORE *VEGETABLES*?"

"YOU CAN GO BACK TO SLEEP, DAD. I'M JUST CHECKIN' MY BATTERIES."

"A MEAN YOUR DAD RAN *SMACK* OVER HER? BOY! AN' BROKE LEGS? AN' MAYBE HER NECK? GEE! YOU'RE GONNA HAVE TO *ANOTHER* DOLL, MARGARET!"

"SOMETIMES YA SAY YA DON'T HEAR ME KNOCK. SO...."

"HERE'S ONE, MARTHA: 'LOVELY, NEW 2-BEDROOM APARTMENT, SUNDECK, BUILT-INS, GARAGE. **NO** CHILDREN....'"

"I THOUGHT MAYBE THEY'D LIKE TO SWIM IN A *LAKE* FOR A CHANGE!"

"..HOWEVER, IF MR. HELMICK CAN *PROVE* DENNIS TOOK HIS CUCKOO, HEREBY LEAVING HIS CUCKOO CLOCK CUCKOOLESS...."

"I *HAD* TO LET THEM IN, GEORGE! THEY FOUND OUT THAT YOU'RE THE ONE WHO'S BEEN SELLING RIFLES TO THE *INDIANS!*"

"HEY, FELLOWS.....WHAT'S A BIKINI?"

"I HOPE THIS DON'T GO EXTRA INNINGS. I'M LIABLE TO GET *SICK!*"

"DON'T WORRY, MR. WILSON! *I'LL* PUT IT OUT!"

"I MADE A *TOUCHDOWN!*"

"GEE WHIZ! I DIDN'T KNOW DAD USED TO BE A *TRAMP!*"

'I THOUGHT I HEARD SOMEBODY *CALLIN'* ME!

"...Y, MOM! COULD WE COME IN AN' GET *COLD?*"

"YA WON'T HEAR ANYTHING FROM 425 MAPLE TONIGHT, 'CAUSE I'M AT THE *SEABREEZE MOTEL!*"

"KAY, ALL SET? NOW, TAKE HOLD OF YOUR OAR, LIKE DADDY
HOLDING *HIS* OAR, AND......"

"OKAY DEWEY. *NOW* WE CAN TALK. I FINALLY GOT EVERYBODY TO SLEEP."

"MY, HE *IS* NEARSIGHTED, ISN'T HE?"

"HEY! YOU'RE PRETTY *FAST!*"

"I HOPE YOU'RE THIS ANXIOUS TO SEE US *RETURN* FROM OUR VACATION, MR. WILSON!"

"GUESS HOW LONG IT TAKES TO MELT A SNOWBALL *THIS BIG* IN THE OVEN!"

"YOU SURE ARE COOKIN' A LOT OF STUFF. I'LL BET WE'VE GOT THE *SMELLIEST* KITCHEN IN THE *WHOLE BLOCK!*"

"SHE *NEVER* PAYS ATTENTION TO ME. I WANTED *CHILI* AN' HOTDOGS AN' ROOTBEER TONIGHT!"

"MILK?! AT A *BIRTHDAY PARTY*?"

"WHEN WE GET HOME, WE'VE GOT A *SURPRISE* FOR MY DAD! MY MOM IS GONNA TELL HIM WHERE SHE HID HIS *GOLF CLUBS!*"

"HEY, MR. HARMON! YA WANNA *SWING* AT A COUPLE?"

"WELL, *I'M* MAD, TOO! I DIDN'T *WANT* A DARN OL' WHITE YO-YO!"

"WHEN I SAY 'GOOD MUSIC' I *CERTAINLY* DON'T MEAN *COWBOY BOB* RECORDS!"

"OH, DIDN'T I TELL YA? I DECIDED TO USE MY UNDERWEAR DRAWER FOR A TOOL CHEST."

"...OMEDAY I MIGHT MEET A KID WHO COLLECTS *LOCKS!*"

"CAN'T YOU KEEP AN EYE ON HIM FOR A FEW DAYS?
HE'S GETTING AHEAD OF ME!"

"I'M SAVIN' UP TO GET *TATTOOED!*"

"LOOK, LADY, HOW 'BOUT LISTENIN' TO *ME* FOR A CHANGE? YOU ALREADY TOLD ME *TEN TIMES* WHAT O'CLOCK IT IS!"

DESSERT THAT I'M BEIN' SENT TO BED WITHOUT.....
D I HAVE IT FOR BREAKFAST?'

"WELL, BE SEEIN' YA, DEWEY. HERE COMES MY HORSE NOW!"

"*LOTS* O' KIDS ARE WORSE 'N ME. BUT YOU DON'T KNOW IT 'CAUSE YOU'RE AN *ONLY MOTHER!*"

"NOPE, THAT DON'T HELP. I *STILL* CAN'T READ!"

"YOU KNOW THAT VASE IN THE OTHER ROOM YOU SAID YOU WERE GONNA GET RID OF SOMEDAY ANYWAY? ...."

"How 'bout puttin' in some money that don't clank?"

"I COULDN'T FIND A WATER GLASS, SO I
OPENED A ROOT BEER. OKAY?"

"HERE'S YOUR PAPER ... 'CEPT THE *FUNNY* ONES. I'M READIN' THEM."

"HI, MR. WILSON! DID YA KNOW THAT WAS *ME* PUNCHIN' YOUR BELL?"

"'MEMBER HOW YOU SAY 'WOW' WHEN YOU LOOK AT THE THERMOMETER, DAD? WELL, IT'S 'WAY _BELOW_ 'WOW' THIS MORNING!"

"CRAZY LITTLE BOY WANTS *CATSUP* ON HIS CHOP SUEY!"

"THAT'S A LIZARD'S TAIL. THE REST OF HIM GOT AWAY."

"TOLD MR. WILSON WE'RE BACK, AN' HE SAID *ALREADY?*"

'HE SAID HE WAS CHECKING TO SEE HOW MANY EARLY BIRDS AND HOW MANY SLEEPYHEADS LIVED IN THIS BLOCK'!'

"YOU ALWAYS SAY 'AMEN' 'CAUSE IT DON'T SOUND
NICE TO SAY 'SO LONG' TO GOD."

"IF YOU'RE GONNA TALK LIKE THAT, MR. WILSON, I'M GONNA HANG YA UP!"

", MR. WILSON! GEE, I DIDN'T KNOW _YOU_ EVER WENT
CHURCH!"

"IT'S A LITTLE GLASS THING THIS LONG. AND IF IT SAYS YOU'RE SICK, YOU'RE *SICK!*"

"I'M THE MAN OF THE HOUSE WHEN MY DAD'S NOT HOME, AN' I DON'T *HEAR* TIES!"

"ANYBODY KNOW WHAT HAPPENED TO THE SANDMAN?"

"ONE THING I'LL SAY FOR HIM: HE'S NOT SELFISH. HE'S GIVEN ME A *LOT* OF THINGS. HEARTBURN, HEADACHES, AN ULCER ...."

"YOU GONNA DIVORCE ME?"

"THE SHORT CARPENTER WANTS TO KNOW IF YOUR WIFE SENT FRIED CHICKEN AGAIN?"

'HI, MOM! I'M SHOWIN' JOEY HOW TO LICK STAMPS!'

"THERE! WASN'T THAT BETTER THAN AN OL' HAIRCUT?"

'*RUFF* STILL LIKES ME!'